A Rookie reader®
TREASURY

Cat in the Bag

and Other
Pet Stories

Children's Press ®
An Imprint of Scholastic Inc.
New York • Toronto • London • Auckland • Sydney
Mexico City • New Delhi • Hong Kong
Danbury, Connecticut

Dear Rookie Reader,

Do you have a dog or cat?
Do you wish that you did?
Then this is the book for you!

Meet a kid with **lots** of cats.
Meet a dog that **likes hats** and
a dog that has **its own pet**.
Then find out how a cat gets
to **take a trip**.

Have fun and keep reading!

P.S. Don't forget to check out the
fun activities on pages 124-127!

Contents

4

Cats!

By Larry Dane Brimner
Illustrated by Tom Payne

Cats!

Come in, cats.

Let's play, cats.

Please, cats!
Stay on the floor.

Don't swing, cats.

Don't fight, cats.

No, cats!
Don't scratch the door.

What's this, cats?
A string, cats.

Catch it, cats—
if you can.

Close, cats.
Almost, cats.

Oh, silly cats!
I love you more and more.

I've Lost My Hat

By Charnan Simon
Illustrated by Rick Stromoski

My hat! My hat!
I've lost my hat!

I cannot find my favorite hat!

I think I've looked
most everywhere.

Under the bed.

Beneath the chair.

Behind the shelf.

On the stairs.

I had it at the park with me.

It fell off when I climbed a tree.

I stuck it in my pocket, and then . . .

I put it on my head again.

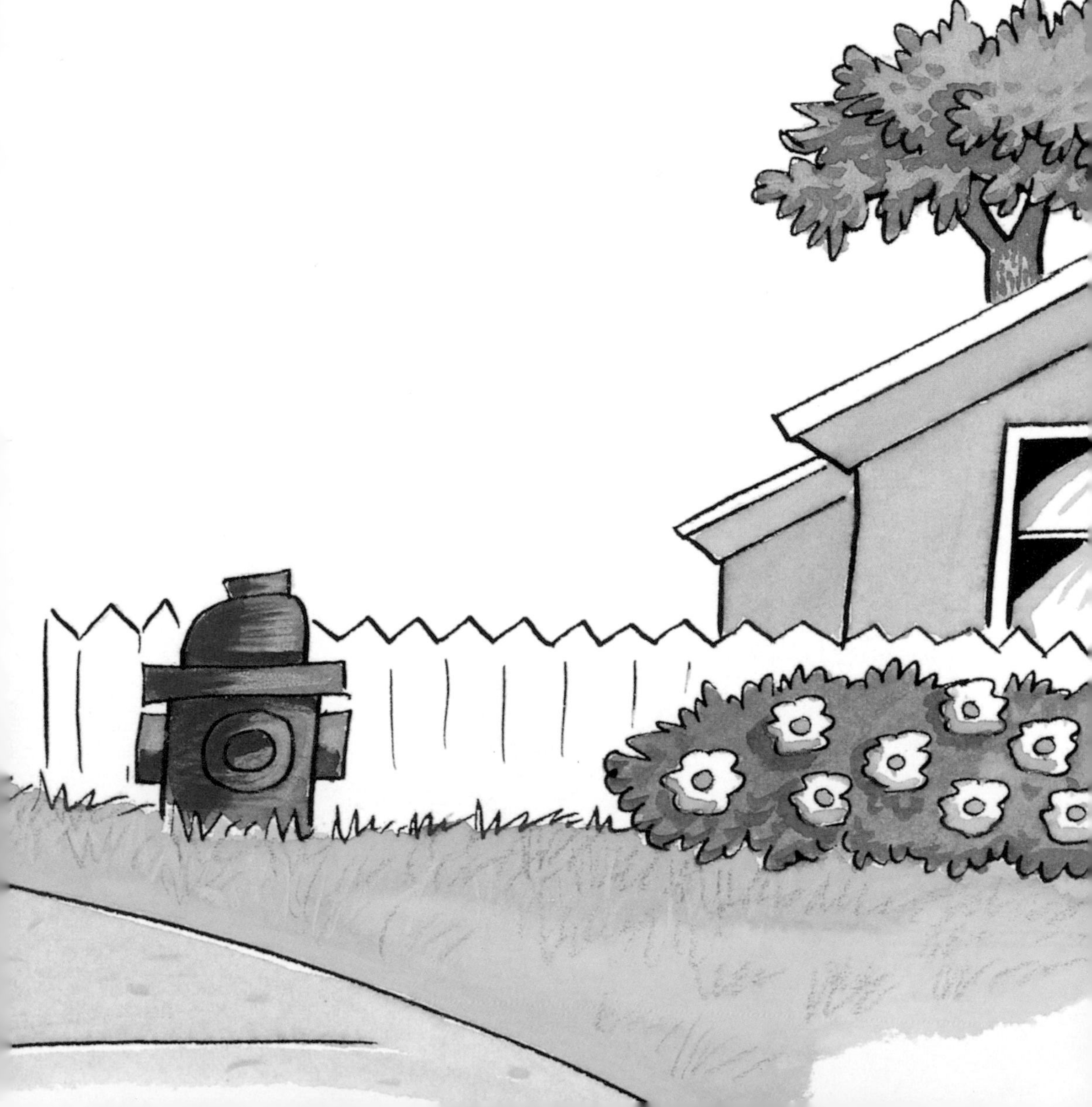

I hung it on the hallway rack when . . .

I came home to eat my snack.

Where did I put it?
Where could it be?

THERE'S my favorite hat!

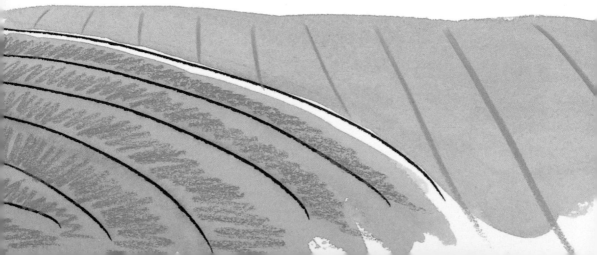

Sam's Pet

By Charnan Simon
Illustrated by Gary Bialke

Rosie and Sam had a new pet.

Her name was Mabel.

Mabel was tiny,

and adorable,

Mabel did not want
to share Sam's food,

or his toys,

or his bed.

Next to Mabel,
Sam felt like a big, dumb dog.

One day,
the neighborhood bully
came over to steal Sam's bone.

Sam never argued with Butch.

But Mabel did.

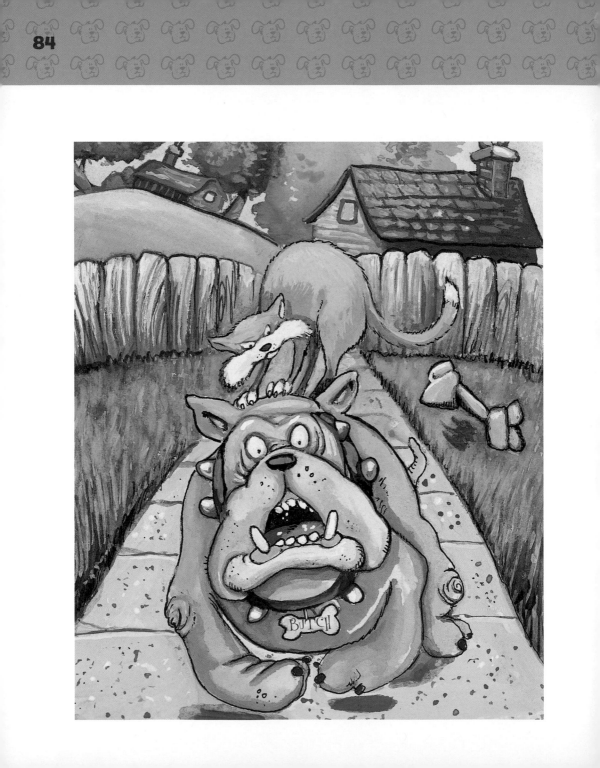

First she took care
of Butch.

Then she took care of Sam.

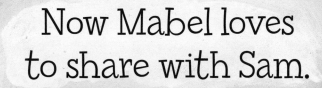

Now Mabel loves to share with Sam.

He's such a pussycat.

Cat in the Bag

By Sara Swan Miller

Illustrated by Benton Mahan

Are you taking a trip?

What will you pack?

One sweater, one jacket,
one scarf, one hat.

No, no!
Not the CAT!

Two shirts, two shoes,
three pants, three caps.

Some socks—four pair.
And yes, underwear!

But NO CATS!
Get out of there!

Five books, six games,
a ball, a toy train.

Some paper, a pen,

and crayons . . .
one, two, three, four, five,
six, seven, eight, nine, ten!

A brush, shampoo,

and the cat?

you come, too!

Rhyme Time

Match the words that rhyme!

catch	stay
door	scratch
play	more

What words rhyme with **swing**?
Hint: there is one clue in this picture.

Complete the sentence with the right word.

The boy found his hat on the _____.
chair   **dog**   **bed**

How did the hat get lost?

Retell the Story!

These pictures are all mixed up!
Tell what happened first, second,
third, and last!

What would you pack
to take on a trip?

Make a list.
Draw a picture, too.

Library of Congress Cataloging-in-Publication Data

Cat in the bag and other pet stories.
    p. cm. -- (A Rookie reader treasury)
  Includes activity pages.
  Contents: Cats! / by Larry Dane Brimner ; illustrated by Tom Payne -- I've lost my hat / by Charnan Simon ; illustrated by Rick Stromoski -- Sam's pet / by Charnan Simon ; illustrated by Gary Bialke -- Cat in the bag / by Sara Swan Miller ; illustrated by Benton Mahan.

  ISBN-13: 978-0-531-20848-9
  ISBN-10: 0-531-20848-6
  1. Children's stories, American. 2. Pets--Juvenile fiction. 3. Animals--Juvenile fiction. [1. Pets--Fiction. 2. Animals--Fiction. 3. Short stories.] I. Title. II. Series.

  PZ5.C1846 2009
  [E]--dc22

                        2008021943